CATS
SET III

Cornish Rex Cats

Julie Murray
ABDO Publishing Company

visit us at
www.abdopub.com

Published by ABDO Publishing Company, 4940 Viking Drive, Edina, Minnesota 55435. Copyright © 2003 by Abdo Consulting Group, Inc. International copyrights reserved in all countries. No part of this book may be reproduced in any form without written permission from the publisher.

Printed in the United States.

Photo Credits: Animals Animals pp. 7, 9, 17, 21; Corbis pp. 5, 19; Peter Arnold pp. 11, 13; Ron Kimball p. 15
Contributing Editors: Tamara L. Britton, Kristin Van Cleaf, Stephanie Hedlund
Book Design & Graphics: Neil Klinepier

Library of Congress Cataloging-in-Publication Data

Murray, Julie, 1969-
   Cornish Rex cats / Julie Murray.
       p. cm. -- (Cats. Set III)
   Summary: Briefly presents information about the curly-coated cat breed that is sometimes referred to as "the poodle cat."
   Includes bibliographical references (p.).
   ISBN 1-57765-863-9
    1. Rex cat--Juvenile literature. [1. Rex cat. 2. Cats.] I. Title.

SF449.R4 M87 2002
636.8'22--dc21
                                                                    2001056726

Contents

Lions, Tigers, and Cats 4

Cornish Rex Cats................................. 6

Qualities... 8

Coat and Color 10

Size 12

Care 14

Feeding 16

Kittens 18

Buying a Kitten 20

Glossary 22

Web Sites... 23

Index 24

Lions, Tigers, and Cats

The first cats lived about 35 million years ago. There are several different types of cats. But they all belong to the animal family **Felidae**. There are 38 different species in this family.

Cats are organized into three different categories. Examples of big cats are lions, tigers, jaguars, and leopards. The small cats include **domestic** cats, lynx, and bobcats. Cheetahs are in a group by themselves.

Domestic cats are believed to be the descendant of the African wildcat. Cats were tamed about 4,000 years ago in Egypt. Today, there are more than 40 different recognized **breeds** of domestic cats.

Big cats such as lions have many of the same characteristics as the Cornish Rex!

Cornish Rex Cats

Cornish Rex cats are easily recognized by their curly, plush coats. For this reason, they are sometimes called the Poodle Cat.

Cornish Rexes were first **bred** in Cornwall, England. In 1950, Nina Ennismore's farm cat had a **litter** of kittens. One of the kittens had curly hair. Ennismore bred the curly-haired kitten with its mother and the Cornish Rex breed was developed.

In 1957, the Cornish Rex arrived in the United States. It was first recognized as an official breed by the **Cat Fanciers' Association** in 1964. Today, they are more popular in the United States than in Europe.

The first Cornish Rex cat was named Kallibunker. All Cornish Rexes, including this one, are related to Kallibunker.

Qualities

Cornish Rex cats are ideal family pets. They are playful, friendly, and good with children. They are energetic, and can be quite vocal at times!

Cornish Rexes quickly become attached to their owners, and they love to be around people. So Cornish Rex cats do not do well when left alone for long periods of time. If you are gone all day, consider getting two of them so they have company.

Some Cornish Rexes will walk on a leash, greet you at the door, and even fetch a small ball. These lovable cats are social, intelligent, and curious.

THE FAY SCHOOL LIBRARY

Cornish Rexes are very energetic and enjoy lots of space to play.

Coat and Color

Most cats have coats that are made up of three different layers of hair. These layers are the long, coarse guard hairs, the finer awn hairs, and the downy **undercoat**.

But Cornish Rexes only have two of these layers. They do not have guard hairs. And they have very short hair. This gives Cornish Rexes their distinctive look.

Cornish Rexes come in many different colors. They can be white, black, blue, red, smoke, tabby, or **tortoiseshell**.

Most Cornish Rexes have gold or green eyes, except for the Si-Rex, which has blue eyes. The color of their nose and paw pads corresponds with their coat color. Cornish Rexes also have short, curly whiskers.

The curls in a Cornish Rex's coat are called Marcel waves. They are named after French hairdresser Marcel Grateau, who invented the waving iron in the 1870s.

Size

    The Cornish Rex is a small to medium-sized cat. Its body is long, slender, and muscular. The male Cornish Rex is often larger than the female.

    The Cornish Rex's back naturally arches, so its underside looks tucked up. Its small, egg-shaped head is longer than it is wide, with prominent cheekbones.

    A Cornish Rex has large ears that are wide at the base and set high on its head. The eyes are oval shaped and slant upward.

    The Cornish Rex has long, slender legs. Its paws have small, oval pads. Its tail is long, thin, and slightly tapered at the end.

The Cornish Rex's high energy level causes it to burn a lot of calories. So most Cornish Rexes are thin cats.

Care

Cornish Rexes are easy to groom. Their short coat hardly sheds at all. They only need to be brushed or combed once a week. A baby brush or fine-toothed comb work well. Avoid overbrushing, which will cause bald spots.

Like any cat, the Cornish Rex will frequently need to sharpen its claws. This is a natural behavior for all cats. Providing a scratching post will save your furniture from damage.

All cats love to play and the Cornish Rex is no different. Movement is important for their enjoyment. So try to provide them with toys that they can move. A ball, a **catnip** mouse, or anything they can move with their paws will be good.

It is a natural instinct for cats to bury their waste. So they should be trained to use a **litter box**. The litter box needs to be cleaned every day. Cats should also be **spayed** or **neutered** unless you are planning on **breeding** them.

Cornish Rexes want to be near their owners and often follow them around the house so as not to miss any action!

Feeding

All cats are **carnivores**. They need food that is high in protein, such as meat or fish. Cats can be very picky and do not like changes in their diet.

Homemade diets usually do not provide the **nutrients** that cats need. A better choice is commercial cat food. It comes in three types. They are dry, semidry, and canned. Each kind offers similar nutritional value.

Dry foods are the most convenient. They can prevent **tartar** buildup on your cat's teeth. Canned foods are the most appealing to cats. But they do not stay fresh for very long.

Cats also need fresh water every day. Your cat may love to drink milk. But many cats are unable to **digest** milk. It will often make them sick. Cats also love treats. You can find many treats at your local pet store.

Cornish Rexes have big appetites. They need a lot of food to fuel their high activity level.

Kittens

    Baby cats are called kittens. Cats are **pregnant** for about 65 days before the kittens are born. Cornish Rexes have three or four kittens per **litter**.

    All kittens are born blind and helpless. They need to drink their mother's milk for the first three weeks. Then they start to eat solid food. Most kittens stop drinking their mother's milk when they are about eight weeks old.

    Kittens start becoming independent when they are about three weeks old. By then they can see, hear, and stand on their own. At about seven weeks, they can run and play. When kittens are 12 weeks old, they can be sold or given away.

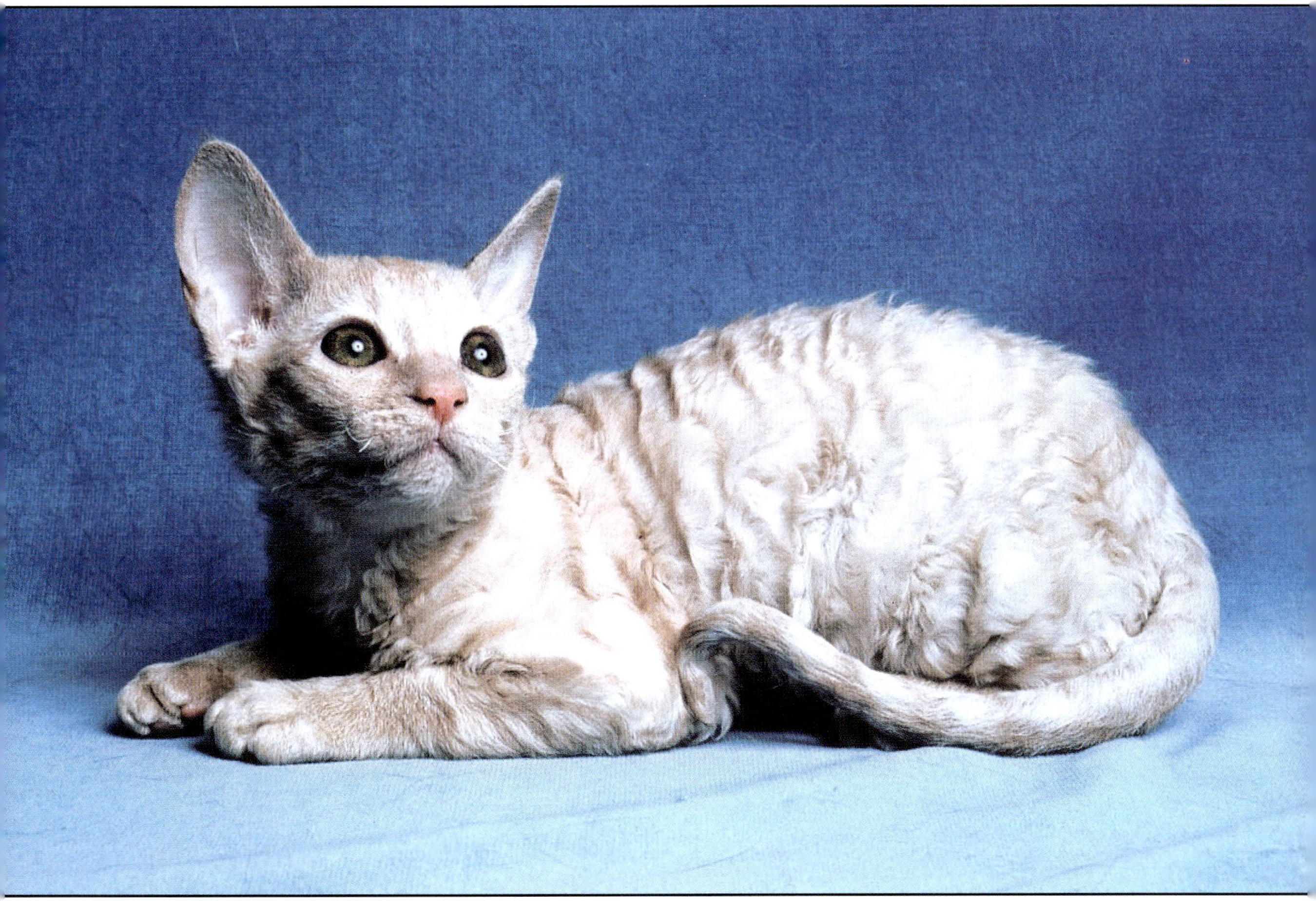

 The Marcel waves in a Cornish Rex's coat are present when it is born. The waves disappear when the kitten is about a week old. But don't worry! The waves will return when the kitten is three to nine months old.

Buying a Kitten

A healthy cat will live about 14 to 16 years. Kittens become very attached to their owners. So before you buy a kitten, be sure you will be able to take care of it for as long as it lives.

There are many places to get kittens. A qualified **breeder** is the best place to buy a **purebred** kitten. When buying from a breeder, be sure to get the kitten's **pedigree** papers and health records. Pet shelters, veterinarians, and cat shows are also good places to find kittens.

When choosing a kitten, check to see that it is healthy. Its ears, nose, mouth, and fur should all be clean. The eyes should be bright and clear. The kitten should be alert and playful.

A Cornish Rex kitten will grow to be an intelligent, attentive, and affectionate companion.

Glossary

breed - a group of cats that shares the same appearance and characteristics. A breeder is a person who raises cats. Raising cats is often called breeding them.
carnivore - an animal or plant that eats meat.
Cat Fanciers' Association - a group that sets the standards for breeds of cats.
catnip - the dried leaves and stems of a plant in the mint family. Catnip is used as a stuffing in cat toys because cats are stimulated by its strong smell.
digest - to break down food in the stomach.
domestic - animals that are tame.
Felidae - the Latin name for the cat family.
litter - all of the kittens born at one time to a mother cat.
litter box - a box where cats dispose of their waste.
neuter - to remove a male animal's reproductive organs.
nutrients - vitamins and minerals that all living things need to survive.
pedigree - a record of an animal's ancestors.

pregnant - having one or more babies growing within the body.

purebred - an animal whose parents are both from the same breed.

spay - to remove a female animal's reproductive organs.

tartar - a crust that forms on the teeth. Tartar is made of saliva, food particles, and salts.

tortoiseshell - a color pattern of blotches of black, orange, and cream.

undercoat - soft, short hair or fur that is partly covered by longer protective hairs.

Web Sites

Would you like to learn more about Cornish Rex cats? Please visit **www.abdopub.com** to find up-to-date Web site links to more information on the Cornish Rex. These links are routinely monitored and updated to provide the most current information available.

Index

A

African wildcat 4

B

big cats 4

C

care 14
Cat Fanciers' Association 6
character 8
cheetahs 4
coat 6, 10, 14, 20
color 10
Cornwall, England 6

D

domestic cats 4

E

Egypt 4
Ennismore, Nina 6
Europe 6

F

Felidae 4
food 16, 17, 18

G

grooming 14

H

health 17, 20
history 4, 6

K

kittens 6, 18, 20

L

life span 20
litter box 15

N

neuter 15

P

pedigree 20
play 8, 14, 18, 20
pregnancy 18

S

scratching post 14
shedding 14
size 12
small cats 4
spay 15

T

teeth 16
training 8, 15

V

voice 8